D0597807

921 WIL

Britton, Tamara L., 1963-
Prince William.

	DATE DUE		

YOUNG PROFILES

Prince William

Tamara L. Britton
ABDO Publishing Company

visit us at
www.abdopub.com

Published by ABDO Publishing Company 4940 Viking Drive, Edina, Minnesota 55435.
Copyright © 1999 by Abdo Consulting Group, Inc. International copyrights reserved in
all countries. No part of this book may be reproduced in any form without written
permission from the publisher.

Printed in the United States.

Photo credits: AP/Wide World; Shooting Star

Edited by Paul Joseph
Contributing editor A.T. McKenna

Library of Congress Cataloging-in-Publication Data

Britton, Tamara L., 1963-
    Prince William / Tamara L. Britton.
    p. cm. -- (Young profiles)
    Includes index.
    Summary: A biography of the popular English prince, whose happiness was
tempered with the divorce of his parents and then by the death of his mother.
    ISBN 1-57765-324-6 (hardcover)
    ISBN 1-57765-336-X (paperback)
    1. William, Prince, grandson of Elizabeth II, Queen of Great Britain, 1982- --
Juvenile literature. 2. Princes--Great Britain--Biography--Juvenile literature.
[1. William Prince, grandson of Elizabeth II, Queen of Great Britain, 1982- .
2. Princes.] I. Title. II. Series.
DA591.A45W553 1999
941.085'092--dc21
    [B]   98-38113
                                              CIP
                                              AC

Contents

An Inspirational Life

Prince William is one of the most popular young people in the world today. He is smart, charming, well-educated, and handsome. He has attended the finest schools. He is a member of the British royal family, and will one day rule the United Kingdom.

The young prince has everything going for him and a bright future. Prince William's happiness, however, has been **tempered** with sorrow. First, his parents decided to **divorce**. Then, he suffered the tragic loss of his mother.

Prince William has handled these challenges with maturity and grace. His ability to maintain good grades in school and **persevere** in the face of such difficulty makes his life story an inspiration to everyone.

Young girls reach for the hand of Prince William as he arrives at a school in Burnaby, B.C., March 24, 1998.

His Royal Highness William of Wales

Name: William Arthur Philip Louis Windsor
Parents: Prince Charles, His Royal Highness the Prince of Wales, and the late Princess Diana
Siblings: Prince Henry Charles Albert David Windsor
Date of Birth: June 21, 1982
Place of Birth: London, England
Height: 6 feet 1/2 inch
Weight: 135 pounds
Eyes: Blue
Hair: Blond
Hobbies: Swimming, Rugby, Skiing, Rowing, Water Polo, Tennis, Hunting, Painting, Reading

Princess Diana hands William his diving mask.

From left to right: Prince Harry, Prince Charles, and Prince William ride the chairlift at Whistler Mountain, Canada.

The Royal Family

The United Kingdom is a constitutional **monarchy**. This means that while the kingdom is governed by a **parliament** and a set of constitutional laws, there is still a king or queen who rules the land.

Usually the title of king or queen of a kingdom is **hereditary**. The crown is passed down through a royal family. Prince William's family is the royal family in the United Kingdom. The United Kingdom includes England, Scotland, Wales, and Northern Ireland. The official home of the royal family is Buckingham Palace in London, England.

Prince William's grandmother, Elizabeth II, is the queen. William's grandfather is Prince Philip. Their son, Prince Charles, is William's father. William also has two uncles, Princes Andrew and Edward, and an aunt, Princess Anne.

Prince Philip and Queen Elizabeth II are Prince William's grandparents.

The Prince's Parents

Prince William's parents are the Prince and Princess of Wales. His father, Prince Charles Philip Arthur George, is the twenty-first prince of Wales. Prince William's mother was Diana, Princess of Wales, the former Lady Diana Spencer.

Prince Charles is **heir** to the British throne. This means that he will be the king of the United Kingdom after Prince William's grandmother, Queen Elizabeth II. Prince Charles attended Trinity **College** at Cambridge University, and was the first heir to the throne to earn a bachelor's degree.

Princess Diana attended private schools in England and Switzerland. She was a kindergarten teacher when she began dating Prince Charles. Soon Charles decided he wanted to marry Diana. He asked her to marry him on February 6, 1981. Diana said yes! The world prepared for a royal wedding.

The Prince and Princess of Wales with their sons, Prince Harry (L)and Prince William in the Sicily Islands in 1989.

A Royal Wedding

Prince Charles and Lady Diana were married on July 29, 1981. They were married at Saint Paul's Cathedral in London, England. Royal weddings usually are held at Westminster **Abbey**. But the Abbey could not hold all of the guests. There were 2,600 people at the wedding!

The wedding was the biggest media event in history. Seven hundred million people watched it on British television. Two hundred and fifty million listened to the wedding on the radio. In all, nearly one billion people witnessed the event in 141 countries all around the world.

After their wedding, Prince Charles and Princess Diana settled down. They had two houses to live in, Kensington Palace and a house in the country called Highgrove. They were a happy couple and started a family right away.

The Prince and Princess of Wales on their wedding day.

Prince William

Prince William Arthur Philip Louis was born on June 21, 1982. He was born at 9:03 P.M. in the Lindo wing at Saint Mary's Hospital near Paddington in London, England. He is the first **heir** to the British throne to be born in a hospital.

Prince William's parents were delighted with him. They even took him along with them on a trip to Australia when he was a baby so they could all stay together. He was a rowdy little boy who was sometimes referred to as the Prince of Wails and His Naughtiness! His parents called him Wills and began to teach him about music and art.

Soon Prince William had a baby brother. Prince Henry Charles Albert David was born on September 15, 1984. Prince William had a happy family. Soon it was time for him to begin school.

The Prince and Princess of Wales with six-month-old Prince William at Kensington Palace on December 22, 1982.

Off to School

William's first day of school was September 24, 1985. He attended nursery school. He is the first **heir** to the throne to attend nursery school instead of being taught at home by a **governess**. In January of 1987, he went on to Weatherby Pre-**Prep School** in Notting Hill.

In September of 1990, William attended Ludgrove Prep School. In 1991, while at Ludgrove, he was hit on the head with a golf club by a fellow student. He was very brave and did not even cry.

William's parents were very concerned. He was taken to the hospital for surgery to correct the indentation the blow left in his head. The surgery lasted more than an hour. Fortunately, all went well and William's head healed perfectly.

Prince William was an excellent student and did well in prep school. After Ludgrove, William was accepted to Eton **College**.

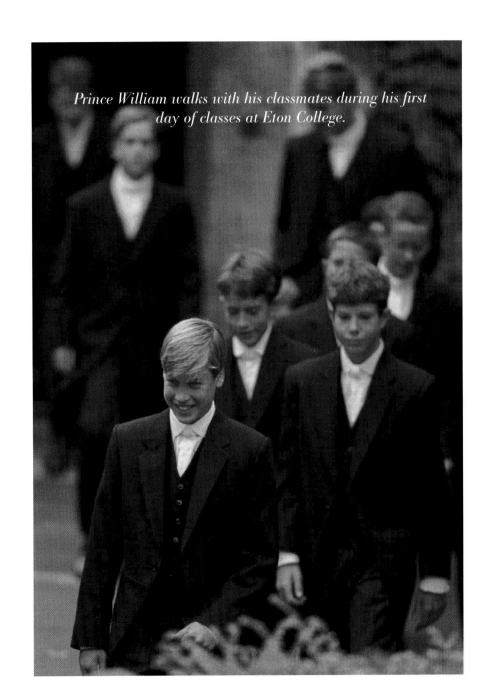

Prince William walks with his classmates during his first day of classes at Eton College.

A Difficult Development

While Prince William was still a student at Ludgrove, he received some disturbing news. His parents, Prince Charles and Princess Diana, had decided to **separate**. Their separation was announced by Buckingham Palace on December 9, 1992.

Prince Charles decided to live at Highgrove, while Princess Diana, William, and Harry lived at Kensington Palace. The Prince attended royal functions, while the Princess devoted her time to various **charities**. They made sure to spend as much time as possible with Prince William and Prince Harry.

But Prince William's parents were not able to resolve their differences, and they decided to get a **divorce**. They were divorced in 1996, the year after William began school at Eton **College**.

William and Harry continued to live with their mother, and spent time with Prince Charles when they could. Prince William's family seemed to be doing as well as possible, when disaster struck.

Prince William signs the traditional entrance book at Eton College, while the Prince and Princess of Wales and Prince Harry look on.

Tragedy in France

On Saturday, August 30, 1997, Princess Diana was in Paris, France. She was having dinner at the Ritz Hotel with her friend Emad "Dodi" al-Fayed.

After dinner, the Princess and her friend wanted to leave the restaurant. But there were many photographers waiting outside who wanted to take pictures of them.

Diana and Dodi did not want their picture taken. They decided to sneak out of a back door to avoid the photographers. Quickly, they left the Ritz and got into a waiting car.

The car sped away, taking Dodi and the Princess away from the photographers. The photographers found out that the Princess and Dodi were in the car, and they followed it, still trying to take pictures.

The driver of the car was driving fast to get away from the photographers. He was driving so fast that he lost control of the car. The car slammed into a post while going through a tunnel. Diana's friend Dodi died right away.

The Princess was rushed to a hospital, where doctors tried to save her life. But her injuries were too severe. Prince William's mother, Princess Diana, died at 4:00 A.M. on Sunday, August 31, 1997.

Prince William, left, and Prince Harry view tributes left in memory of their mother Princess Diana.

A Special Funeral

Prince William learned of his mother's death while dressing for church that Sunday morning. He was close to his mother and was sad to lose her. Prince William, Prince Charles, and Prince Harry prepared for her funeral.

Princess Diana's body was sent from France to England on an airplane. The funeral was held on Saturday, September 6, 1997, in London, England.

The funeral service for William's mother was as big an event as her wedding had been 16 years earlier. About 2,000 guests filled Westminster **Abbey** to pay their last **respects** to the Princess. Around 31 million people watched the services on television in England and in 230 other countries.

From left to right:
Earl Charles Spencer, Prince William, Prince Harry, and Prince Charles at the funeral of Princess Diana.

After the funeral, Princess Diana was taken from Westminster Abbey to Althorp, her family's home, to be buried. Prince William, along with his father, his brother, his grandfather, and his uncle, walked along behind the carriage that carried his mother to her final resting place. He was very sad, but still managed to smile at some of his countrymen who grieved with him and his family. Even in his time of sorrow, Prince William was able to think of others. His mother was buried on a small island in a lake on her family's estate.

The casket bearing the body of Princess Diana is taken into Westminster Abbey. Standing with backs to camera are from left, Prince Charles, Prince Harry, Princess Diana's brother Earl Charles Spencer, and Prince William.

The Young Prince

After the death of his mother, Prince William found **solace** with his family. He is close to his father and brother. He sees Prince Harry often and spends time with Prince Charles as often as possible. Prince William also visits his grandparents a lot.

Prince William has continued his studies at Eton **College**. He studies geography, biology, and art history to prepare him to enter a university. He is a skilled artist. One of his drawings was chosen for display at his school.

After Prince William finishes at Eton, he will continue his education. He has not decided which university he will attend. But whichever school he picks, William is already well on his way to being a **competent** and **compassionate** king.

Prince Charles (C) and his two sons Prince William (L) and Prince Harry (R), take an early morning walk along the banks of the River Dee.

The Future King

Prince William will one day be the king of England. He will rule England, Scotland, Wales, and Northern Ireland. He will head the Commonwealth, a group of countries that is associated with the British Empire. William will also be the head of the Church of England, and Commander-in-Chief of the armed services.

Though England is governed by a prime minister and **parliament**, Prince William will have the power to **veto** bills before they become law. He will receive visitors, see diplomats, meet government officials, and heads of **charities**.

While this is a lot of responsibility, Prince William will be ready to be the king. With his father's sense of duty and his mothers sense of charity, William could be one of the best kings the United Kingdom has ever had.

Opposite page: Prince William during a visit to Vancouver, Canada, June 1998.

Fun Facts About Prince William

- Prince William has a Labrador retriever named Widgeon.
- Prince William learned to read when he was five years old and likes fiction, nonfiction, and poetry.
- When Prince William was born, his father was in the delivery room with Princess Diana. It was the first time ever that the father was present at a royal birth.
- Prince Charles is distantly related to George Washington, and Princess Diana was related through her mother to both John Adams and Franklin Delano Roosevelt. That makes Prince William related to them, too!
- At more than six feet tall, Prince William is already taller than both of his parents.

Prince William during a vacation in the Swiss ski resort of Klosters in 1998.

Glossary

Abbey: a church.

Charities: institutions or organizations that give gifts to those in need.

College: a private preparatory or high school in England. A college is also a school in a university.

Compassionate: being sensitive to the feelings of others.

Competent: having adequate abilities and qualifications.

Divorce: an act that legally ends a marriage.

Governess: a person who cares for and instructs children in a private household.

Heir: someone who is entitled to receive something from a parent or predecessor.

Hereditary: something transferred from parents to offspring.

Monarchy: a government with a hereditary chief who has varying degrees of power.

Parliament: an assembly of lords and commoners that is the supreme legislative body in the British government.

Persevere: to persist in the face of discouragement or opposition.

Prep School: a private preparatory school that prepares children for upper levels of education.

Respects: special attention.

Separate: when two married people decide to stay married but to live in different houses.

Solace: a source of relief.

Tempered: to be hardened by something.

Veto: the power of a president or king to reject a bill and keep it from becoming law.

Internet Sites

www.geocities.com/SouthBeach/Lights/9536/William.html
If you are looking for a Prince William "teen-idol" type site jammed with photos, you've come to the wrong place. The focus of this site is on celebrating Prince William the person and social icon, not the pinup boy.

www.gilmer.net/royalty/
Not only will you learn the newest and most interesting information on the future king of England but you will also learn about the history of the royal British family. There are recommended reading lists, great photos, and even audio of Prince William!

These sites are subject to change.

Pass It On

Tell readers around the country information you've learned about your favorite superstars. Share your little-known facts and interesting stories.
We want to hear from you!
To get posted on the ABDO Publishing Company Web site, E-mail us at "Adventure@abdopub.com"
Download a free screen saver at www.abdopub.com

Index